This Inspiring L

C000301646

_____

If found please email me at:

_____

My top three priorities in life are:

1 _____
_____

2 _____
_____

3 _____
_____

My vocation/living my life on purpose
is as follows:

_____
_____
_____
_____

TOP TIPS FOR INSPIRING LEADERS

The Pocket Book of Wisdom

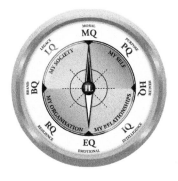

Leigh Bowman-Perks &
Jonathan Bowman-Perks MBE

Fisher King Publishing

TOP TIPS FOR INSPIRING LEADERS

Fisher King Publishing Ltd,
The Studio,
Arthington Lane,
Pool in Wharfedale,
LS21 1JZ,
England.

Cartoons by Roger Penwill

A CIP catalogue record of this book is available
from the British Library
ISBN 978-1-910406-56-4

www.fisherkingpublishing.co.uk

Contents

IL-INSPIRING LEADERSHIP

BE AN INSPIRING LEADER. DRAW OUT THE BEST
THINKING AND ENERGY FROM YOUR TEAM

About this book

We always encourage our leaders to keep things simple. Consequently, in this book, we are practicing what we preach! We want to help you become an even more successful and inspiring leader, yet with less effort. By sharing some of the wisdom that we have collected from our research, and whilst coaching developing leaders, you can tap into some of their most valued practical tools and techniques. Like them, you can then apply these immediately to make a real difference in your performance.

This is your personal, practical pocket book. Here you can take your own and others' wisdom and learning and transform it into actions for you and your team.

All profits from this book go to our Charity – The Inspiring Leadership Trust – for disadvantaged women and children in the UK and around the world. Further information is available if you wish to get involved at:

www.inspiringleadershiptrust.com

Using this book

This book is divided into three parts:

How Best to Use This Book

In this pocket book of wisdom there is a wealth of material to absorb, reflect on and apply to your own leadership. It is a very rich meal; it is not advised to consume it in one sitting. To do so would be like trying to drink from a fire hydrant. This is a book that is intended to help you:

1. Jog your memory

2. Dip into for a specific leadership dilemma you are seeking to resolve.

3. As your daily reference book to carry in your pocket or bag with you on your travels.

Other leaders said about this pocket book, "We valued such a short, snappy selection of profound thoughts. On reading each tip we needed to stop, reflect and think about what they mean to our own leadership context."

Leigh & Jonathan Bowman-Perks MBE

Overview of Inspiring Leadership

Our research shows that the Inspiring Leadership compass directly correlates with performance and potential. Developing your skills and behaviours in any of the 8 components will make a significant impact on your own and others' lives and that of your organisation.

Inspiring Leaders' Practical Tips and Tools

We have consolidated the tips under each of the 8 Inspiring Leadership Principles around the compass. Please use the books as you wish – either from start to finish or dip in anywhere.

Your Personal Action Plan

It's all about transforming your learning into action. Write down your SMART actions (Specific, Measurable, Achievable, Results-orientated and Time-bound). These will help you to create the necessary laser-like focus and absolute commitment in order to be more successful. We have added questions and space for you to add your own learning throughout this pocket book.

> If IQ accounts for 6% of a leader's performance, and EQ contributes to 30%, then what's in the missing 64%?
>
> *Reuven Bar-On, 50 Years of Research into EQ*

About Inspiring Leadership…

it's not about role or title, it is a way of being with others, so they willingly trust and follow you.
It is a leadership performance philosophy and mind-set based on many years of experience and research. This is drawn from our own work in all sectors of global business, Jonathan's experience as a leader and instructor for 20 years in the British Army and research from our mentor and friend Dr Reuven Bar-On.

Inspiring Leaders...

breathe life into others through their energy, passion, gravitas, presence, integrity and trust-worthiness. They have a strong moral compass, clear sense of what gives their lives meaning and purpose and always consider what will leave a sustainable legacy after they have finished their role. They create a healthy culture through being physically and mentally fit, combined with a robustness and grit to learn from setbacks and adversity. They are humble enough to be willing to learn from coaches, mentors and colleagues. In particular they use their emotions intelligently so that they work for them as well as reading and managing others well. They have a strong reputation and track record for successfully delivering business performance through the high levels of engagement of others.

Expiring Leaders & Mis-Leaders...

are the polar opposite of Inspiring Leaders. Their qualities are grandiosity and exaggerated self-worth, pathological lying, manipulation, lack of remorse, shallowness, and exploitation for financial gain. They leave a trail of disaster and mayhem in their wake. At their best they are ineffectual in both their relationships and work; draining the life energy from others. At their most extreme they are Narcissistic, "White Collar Psychopaths". They fail to consider others; it's all about ego, self-advancement and doing whatever it takes to get their way. In their world of altered reality, white-collar psychopaths believe that their performance and contribution drive success, however, it actually destroys the contribution of their teams and the confidence of individuals around them. At all costs they must be challenged and rooted out from your organisation.

MQ – MORAL INTEGRITY

DO YOU CHALLENGE TOXIC BEHAVIOURS, OR ARE YOU JUST A BYSTANDER TO THEM?

MQ – Morals and Integrity

MQ

Role Archetype: Corporate Conscience

Courageous
Morals
Non-Judgmental
TRUST
CHARACTER
HUMILITY
Authenticity
Beliefs
INTEGRITY
Discerning
Risk Savvy
Values
Transparency
RESPONSIBLE

You live life according to a clear set of principles, values and beliefs that guide your decisions, choices and actions. You try to do the right thing at work and in the community. This has been referred to as work ethics, professionalism and moral intelligence.

MQ – Top Tips

1. **Courageous Leadership**
   Having courageous conversations and carrying out courageous acts are the mark of a truly inspiring leader. Consider an inspiring leader who you view as having high integrity and being courageous; what would they do in your situation?

2. **Willful Blindness**
   If you don't challenge dishonesty, lack of integrity and injustice, then you are a bystander. As such you are condoning toxic behaviour. Have the courage to stand by your convictions and do the right thing. Do not be wilfully blind.

3. **What Matters Most?**
   Our lives are often packed with too many things going on simultaneously. We all have the same number of hours in the day. Choose wisely, according to your values, your top 3 life and top 3 work priorities and build clear boundaries. Then the less important, but necessary things can be built around these "big rocks".

4. **Always Be Where You're Indispensable**
    As you continually strive to balance your work and your non-work life, then remember that there are certain events that only you can attend, such as special family moments. Therefore, train up your deputy and delegate more so that you can always be where you're indispensable.

5. **How Much Is Enough?**
    Sara Hart asks many astute questions such as, "How will you know when you have enough?" and "If you knew you already had enough, how would you behave then?"

6. **Character Vs Environment**
    If we make mistakes, then we tend to blame the environment in which we are working, rather than any character defect in ourselves. However, if somebody else makes a mistake, then we blame it on their character defect and lack of integrity, rather than their challenging environment. Apply wise judgement, yet avoid being judgmental.

7. **The Empty Chair**
    When in a one-to-one or team meeting,

always have an empty chair to encourage ethical decision-making. This could represent a key absent stakeholder such as your customer, regulator, or other stakeholder. Then you can ask a colleague, "how would you respond to (a person sitting in the empty chair) if they said…"

8. **The Pragmatic Approach To Leadership**
If you are acting with integrity, in a slow, bureaucratic organisation with little empowerment, then you can become overly cautious. Alternatively, take the pragmatic approach to leadership: "It is far better to beg forgiveness afterwards, than to ask permission beforehand!"

9. **Organisational Saboteurs**
Do you have a colleague who is "an organizational saboteur?" Do they say, "Yes" to requests and instructions, but then do the complete opposite? Do they deliberately undermine their peers, or boss? Are they cynical, believe they "know it all" and act in a passively aggressive manner? If so, then it is time to help them re-recruit themselves and re-commit to the team, or encourage them to

swiftly leave!

10. **If Trust Is Gone, Then They Must Go Too**
    If you don't trust people, you cannot work
    with them, nor for them. Toxic people affect
    everyone. If trust is lost and, despite your
    best efforts, it cannot be rebuilt, then it is
    time to part company. Always be firm in the
    decision and kind in the execution when you
    fire someone.

11. **Be Integrated Not Dis-Integrated**
    When there is congruence and alignment
    between who you are being, your values
    and beliefs, the work you are doing and
    the life you are living, then you are living
    with integrity. To do otherwise leads you to
    become dis-integrated, lack authenticity and
    trustworthiness.

12. **Integrity + Transparency = Trust**
    Inspiring leaders build trusted environments,
    where people feel engaged. This is based
    on their consistently espoused values and
    transparent communication. One of the
    biggest derailers to enabling change is when
    leaders 'protect' people from the truth.

Treating employees as adults demonstrates respect and greater trust.

13. **Trustworthiness**
The most powerful underlying value that defines a leader's success, or failure, is whether other people consider them to be trustworthy. Steven Covey uses the equation Trust = Speed x Cost. When there are high levels of trust between people then things happen very fast and cheap. Otherwise with no or low levels of trust, interactions are painfully slow and highly expensive.

14. **Authenticity vs Flexibility**
It's a fine judgement call to move down the spectrum from being totally authentic, according to your own values and beliefs, versus being more culturally flexible to the norms and culture of the organisation you work in. Find the balance between listening to others' views and sharing your own. Choose your battles carefully and sensitively.

15. **Right But Dead**
Having strong values and principles are

essential to inspiring leaders. However, you also need to be pragmatic and realistic to avoid being "right but dead." Being stubborn at the wrong moment may be fatal. One unwise example is continuing to drive at speed at an oncoming fast car that has crossed over to your side of the road. You are right. They are wrong. You are dead.

16. **Stand Up To Be Counted – Avoid Dante's Hell**
"The darkest places in Hell are reserved for those who maintain their neutrality in time of crisis."

Leigh & Jonathan Bowman-Perks MBE

MQ Questions For You

1. What are your top 6 values, beliefs and principles you live your life by?

2. With that in mind what do you need to say, "Yes" to and "No" to more often in your work and life?

MQ Your Learning & Action

PQ – MEANING AND PURPOSE

LIVE YOUR LIFE **ON** PURPOSE (RATHER THAN **OFF** PURPOSE)
BY BEING AUTHENTICALLY YOURSELF.

PQ – Meaning and Purpose

PQ

Role Archetype: Strategic Visionary

MEANING

Strategic SUCCESS MEASURES PURPOSE Plan FOCUSED DELIVERY Inspire Vision Long-Term Accountable

Leigh & Jonathan Bowman-Perks MBE

PQ – Top Tips

17. **Living Your Life On Purpose**
    Are you truly "living a life on purpose", rather than "off purpose"? What does it mean to you to have "a life truly well-lived?"

18. **Purpose – Why?**
    Many can explain <u>what</u> they do and <u>how</u> they do it, but they forget to clarify the powerful reason <u>WHY</u>. People will engage when they understand and buy into the 'why' you do what you do. For example, if the organisers of a meeting can't explain its purpose, then don't attend.

19. **Balcony Vs Dance-Floor**
    Get off the dance floor and get up onto the balcony. Then you will be able to see the big picture and make your 3 strategic, value-adding decisions for this year. Avoid micromanagement; encourage your reports to have empowered execution to take action themselves.

20. **2-Up, 1-Up And My Part In Their Plan**
Always consider the requirements of your boss 2 levels up, 1 level up and your part in delivering that success. Be clear on what <u>they</u> define as your purpose and success criteria. Capture your boss's Success and Satisfaction criteria on just 1 Page.

21. **Main Effort (ME) Subsidiary Effort (SE) & Tertiary Effort (TE)**
Historically military success comes from a crystal clear focus and clear sense of mission/purpose. Choose your Main Effort (ME) onto which you put the majority and best of your people, resources and focus. Either side of your ME you have your SE and TE. You therefore have only 3 priorities; one of which is clearly labelled your ME. If your ME is blocked, then switch your best resources to the SE or TE and now re-label that as your ME and reclassify the others.

22. **Focus**
Check – do you have a personal vision to live your life on purpose? Have you a laser-like focus on what matters and what you are doing that adds true value? Avoid dissipating

your energy by spreading yourself too thinly.

23. **Apportion Time According To Your Priorities**
Decide what your ideal week is like and
how you should apportion your finite time
to achieve your Main Effort and Subsidiary
Efforts. Then make a pie chart of how you
have actually allocated your time every week.
Is it congruent? Are you spending far too
much time on things that had little value?

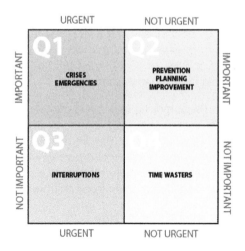

24. **Urgent Vs Important**
Steven Covey has some great tips. One is "the things which matter most should not be at the expense of things which matter least!" A sense of urgency can be addictive and make us feel powerful and useful, but may not add value. Be proactive and focus on the important, not just the urgent aspects of your role.

25. **Look Forwards vs In The Rearview Mirror**
Leading strategically is like driving a sports car on the motorway. You do need to glance occasionally in the rearview mirror to learn from what has happened in the past; however, 90% of your time should be spent looking forward and planning.

26. **Drive - The Surprising Truth About What Motivates People**
Daniel Pink highlights that, instead of money, it is autonomy, mastery and purpose that takes people from mere compliance to greater self-direction and commitment.

27. **Follow Your Passion/Joy/Love**
Work out what gives you true joy, happiness

and produces a resonant vibration within you. This is when you are "in flow" doing what you love doing and performing at the top of your game. When you know what gives you bliss, then follow it. Anything less is a compromise.

28. **Internally Or Externally Controlled?**
You need to seriously consider whether you are the creator of your life or you are passively responding to it. As the creator, then you are the cause and your life is the effect. When you are passive, then the world is the cause of what happens to you and you are affected by it. Choose to be the cause and not the effect of your life. Be proactive not reactive - take control of your life; don't just be controlled by external events.

29. **Beware Upward Delegation**
If you have a culture where everyone delegates upwards to you, then it's your fault. That's because you've created a lack of trust that prevents your subordinates from being able to think for themselves, get on, feel empowered and make things happen. Stop being a control freak; instead coach

and bring on those you lead.

30. **Burning Issues**
At the end of every meeting give every person a quick 30 seconds to share any burning issues. These are topics that have not yet been discussed, but are crucial to address at the next meeting.

31. **The Top 3 Value-Adding Tasks**
As a daily discipline, at the end of the day capture the top 3 tasks that you should perform the next day. These must add the most value to your job. Then first thing in the morning put them in priority order. Then begin with priority 1 and don't give up until you've completed it, before you move onto priority 2 and then onto 3.

32. **Commitment, Or Merely Compliance?**
Check with yourself and those you lead whether they are fully committed to your organisation, the idea, or change proposed, or whether they are just ticking boxes and only complying in a half-hearted way. Tap into what each individual needs to build commitment, rather than making

assumptions, or ignoring that you have dissent in the ranks.

33. **The 2 Most Important Days in Your Life**
Mark Twain wisely said, "The 2 most Important days in your life are the day you were born and the day you found out why". What is your life purpose and why were you born?

PQ Questions For You

1. What gives your life and your work meaning and purpose?

2. According to Mark Twain's quote – have you yet found out why you were born?

Leigh & Jonathan Bowman-Perks MBE

PQ Your Learning & Action

BE A CORPORATE ATHLETE. CHANGE YOURSELF AND DON'T WALLOW IN A TOXIC CULTURE.

HQ – Health and Well-Being

HQ

Role Archetype: Healthy Energiser

Wellbeing
Self-Belief
Emotions Management
HEALTH
Self-Management
PHYSICAL FITNESS
BALANCE
Positive
Attitude
CULTURE
Nutrition

HQ – Top Tips

34. **Your Personal And Organisational Health**
You need your organisation to be lean, fit, resilient and dynamic. It follows that, as a leader, you need to be the same. What can you do to significantly increase your personal energy and vitality?"

35. **Do something about it!**
Adopt John F. Kennedy's wise saying embodied by Amnesty International, "better to light a candle than to curse the darkness." Take action rather than criticise.

36. **Let Go of Resentment**
Take heed of Nelson Mandela's saying: "Resentment is like drinking poison and then hoping it will kill your enemies." And the other saying, "Resentment is like letting someone you dislike live rent free in your head."

37. **10-10-10 Perspective**
You need to get the perspective of time, especially when you are so deep in the

Leigh & Jonathan Bowman-Perks MBE

problem that you "cannot see the wood for the trees". Ask yourself, "How important will this problem be firstly in 10 hours time, then in 10 months time and ultimately in 10 years time?"

38. **Words Create Worlds**
Take care over what you say; it will subliminally shape the way you think and behave. As Henry Ford said, "Whether you think you can, or whether you think you can't, you're probably right!" Your attitude will define your altitude.

39. **Relative Deprivation**
Be careful about constantly comparing yourself to other leaders and groups, putting them on a pedestal. Giving increased status to others relative to yourself can be unhealthy, demoralising and may erode your confidence. Value your own strengths and talents, rather than making everything relevant to what others have.

40. **Your Physiology Shapes Your Leadership Impact**
Make connections with others to generate the hormone oxytocin. Keeping fit and

healthy will also generate endorphins, dopamine and serotonin. Work on staying calm and adopt a positive mental attitude to generate DHEA, the vitality hormone. Negative emotions and thoughts will generate Cortisol, the stress hormone.

41. **Eagles Or Turkeys?**
Do you help your team members soar like eagles - in their own patch of clear blue sky and returning to the communal nest at the end of the day? Or do you treat them like turkeys - stuck under the spotlight in everyone else's ammonia, packed together, with no room to breathe or move in your barn? Empowering your team creates a healthy environment.

42. **Go Easy On Yourself**
Perfectionists are highly self-critical. The problem is that you then hold other people to the same exacting standards and are more critical of people around you. Look for the good in others, catch them doing things right. Rather than constantly striving and doing, just be present with them more often. Create more time to think and re-gather your

resources ready for the next big challenge.

43. **Laughter Is The Best Medicine**
Don't take yourself too seriously; no one else
does! Ask yourself "does this bring joy, love
and happiness to my life and am I having
fun?" If the answer is no, then stop doing it!
You always have a choice; focus more on
what you love and your unique talents.

44. **What Is Your Healthiest Calling/ Job?**
What really should you be doing as
the healthiest job for yourself? Draw 3
overlapping circles. In the 1st circle write
words that capture what you love doing. In
the 2nd circle write down words that capture
your unique talents. In the 3rd one write down
words that capture what the market wants
and will pay for. At the intersection of the 3
circles is what Jack Welch called your zone
of destiny and your ideal calling/job."

45. **You're In The Energy Business**
As an inspiring Leader, you need to energise
and inspire yourself first, before you can
energise anyone else to willingly follow you,
or be influenced by you. They in turn will

give 20-30% more discretionary life energy to the organisation and most importantly your customers, who will consequently come back for repeat business.

46. **Ratio: Done To Me Vs Done By Me**
It is far healthier (mentally) when you have control of your own life and destiny, rather than have things being done to you without you being able to stop or influence them. Equally, the same is true for the people you lead: give them more autonomy.

47. **White Collar Psychopaths & Toxic Leaders**
Toxic leaders hide their vulnerability, fail to have open and honest conversations with you, cannot be trusted, or relied upon and are dysfunctional. Beware of their cold, rather than warm, empathy and lack of genuine emotional connection with you. You are not able to change their behaviour, so insulate and protect yourself from them. Record and evidence all your interactions. Be courageous, act with integrity and get them out of the organisation.

48. **Toxic Teams**
Toxic, dysfunctional teams lack a sense of purpose, direction, loyalty, or values. In the absence of good leadership, they fall back on criticising everyone else, failing to accept personal responsibility, undermining their colleagues and wallowing in gossip. The antidote is to provide clarity, direction and accountability that models collaboration and healthy behaviours. Identify and remove the 'bad apples' that corrupt others and undermine the performance of the business.

49. **Be Resilient, Without Being Stupid**
As we will discuss later in the section on RQ, it is important to cope well with adversity, setbacks and disappointment, and have a high level of resilience. However, it is essential to know when it's time to replenish, renew, refresh and rest. If you do not learn how to self-manage and limit yourself, then it will disastrously affect your health and well-being.

50. **Eat Move Sleep**
Tom Rath advises how small choices in how you exercise, eat and sleep lead to big

changes in your life. You will have far more energy for work and non-work elements of your life. High performers on average have 8 hours and 36 minutes quality sleep a night - I'm sure too many of us have never consistently achieved that yet.

51. **Rewire Your Brain for Success**
Our friend the psychologist Merissa Peer in her TEDx talk said "First you make your beliefs, then your beliefs make you. Make the unfamiliar familiar and the familiar unfamiliar. Choose to link pleasure to the things you want and pain to being stuck in an unhealthy behaviour/place."

HQ Questions For You

1. In what ways can you become physically and mentally healthier?

2. Is your work environment healthy or toxic and what are your going to do about it and the toxic people you may work with?

HQ Your Learning & Action

IQ - WISDOM AND JUDGEMENT

CREATE STRATEGIC THINKING TIME IN ORDER
TO MAKE BETTER DECISIONS

IQ – Cognitive Intelligence and Wisdom

Leigh & Jonathan Bowman-Perks MBE

IQ – Top Tips

52. **Think**
    You are paid to think, not to be busy -
    shorten your meetings to make thinking
    space.

53. **Generate Your Own Wisdom Team**
    Gather around you your own virtual and real
    team of experts and advisers; your wisdom
    team. Accumulate your own coach, mentors,
    friends and advisors; people whom you
    can turn to in order to help your own finest
    thinking and decision-making.

54. **Giants Not Dwarfs**
    Surround yourself with a truly high
    performing team. Recruit and develop a
    metaphorical army of giants - people who
    (in their own specialist areas) are bigger and
    taller then you and far more talented. You can
    then have time to really think at the strategic
    level, be on the balcony, and make yourself
    available for promotion on to even more
    demanding roles. Sadly, too many people
    surround themselves with metaphorical

dwarfs, who are less talented than them and pose no threat, or challenge.

55. **The 5 P's**
   Planning and Preparation Prevents Poor Performance. The military have a maxim, "Time spent in preparation: is never wasted". Lack of planning and preparation (on your behalf as the chair) before a meeting should not become a crisis for the people who work for you. You spend time to save them time.

56. **Monkeys**
   People bring you problems – metaphorical monkeys on their backs. Their aim is to transfer these monkeys onto your back, or leave them in your office, and then get away quickly. Take a Coach-Approach to Leadership by asking them great questions, so they keep their own monkeys and take away one of yours too.

57. **40-Minute Meetings**
   Neuroscience research has shown that our brains tire quickly, so after no more than 40 minutes, take a 5-minute break and leg stretch and then start a new topic.

58. **Agenda Questions**
Turn your agenda items into agenda item questions starting with a "what" or "how" prefix - this will give people time in the lead up to the meeting to gather their thoughts.

59. **Dump It And Be Present**
If you or other people have just rushed in from another meeting, without sufficient time to process what has been going on, then you need 2 minutes to dump or action those thoughts. This quiet moment allows them to jot down thoughts and actions from their last meeting, which they can pick up when they finish your meeting. Then they will be fully present with what you need to achieve.

60. **Sharpen The Saw**
Stephen Covey tells the story of a man in a wood sawing through a large tree. You ask him, "how long have you been doing that?" to which he replies, "3 hours and it is such hard work! I may never get this job done!" You then ask him, "Why don't you stop and sharpen the saw? To which he replies, "Can't you see, stupid? - I haven't got time - I'm too busy sawing through the tree!"

61. **40 Days To Embed Behavioural Change**
Neuroscientists, like our friend Dr Jeff Bird, know that it takes 40+ days of continual practice to embed a change in leadership behaviour. Like going to the gym - 1 session never sustains the change.

62. **Your Best Friend**
When you have a deeply personal problem that is keeping you awake at night, try taking the perspective of someone you trust, such as your best friend. Imagine that your best friend has exactly the same problem as you have now. Then write down what advice you would give your best friend. Now take that good advice yourself.

63. **Living Above The 45°**
Draw a simple graph with an X and Y-axis. Label the Y-axis "my challenges/opportunities" and the X-axis "my abilities". When you live on the 45° line between the two Axes, then your abilities match your challenges exactly - that is a comparatively easy and comfortable place. If, however, you live above the 45° then you will find you are stretched and challenged because

you're in the space of fear, of not knowing, of potentially being wrong. Most importantly (as Nancy Kline advises) that is the place where your greatest growth and learning will happen.

64. **The One Log In The Logjam**
Picture this image and metaphor. When Canadian timber firms send their huge logs speeding down the fast flowing rivers, on their way to the sawmills, they can pile-up on sharp bends. The job of 1 specialist "log-jam man' is to identify the critical 1 log in a pile of up to 200, then fire a harpoon into it and rapidly winch it out, in order to let the whole logjam race on again down the river. Do the same with your problems.

65. **Listen To Your Head, Heart, Gut And Wallet**
We have 89 Billion neurons in our brain, 40,000 in our Heart and 100 Million in our Gut (mini brains). Listen to your head, heart, gut and wallet (finances) and keep tuned into your instinct for being alert to deceit, danger and "things that seem too good to be true" – they nearly always are too good and <u>not</u> true!

66. **Ask "How?" Not "Why?"**
    Start asking how as well as asking why.
    "How?" questions move you to your
    intended future target state in practical steps.

67. **Positive Vs Negative Commands**
    The human mind responds best to clear
    commands. Tell your brain what you want
    (your self talk), not what you don't want.
    It has problems with negatives and losing
    things. Eg telling a child "don't <u>touch</u> the hot
    stove" – they don't hear the negative part of
    your command and still touch it. To get fitter,
    give yourself a target weight, rather than
    saying "lose X weight".

68. **Pre-Mortum - Scenario Planning**
    Imagine you are 12 months on and the
    plan you have just come up with has
    fundamentally failed. What was it that you
    did that went wrong? Now plan strategies to
    mitigate those risks, before they are likely to
    emerge.

69. **Results Only Work Environment (ROWE)**
    Focus on the results of the people you lead,
    rather than presenteeism, attending meetings

and clocking-in and clocking-out of a set work environment. Give them 20% of their weekly time to develop new ideas, which add true value to your organisation beyond their day-to-day jobs.

70. **KISS**
KISS = Keep It Simple Stupid. To paraphrase Albert Einstein, "Everything should be as simple as possible, but no simpler." Leaders make the complex clearer, simpler and easier for everyone to understand and act upon. Philosopher Henry David Thoreau said, "Simplify, simplify, simplify", to which Ralph Waldo Emerson replied, "I think 1 would have sufficed!"

71. **10,000 Hours / 10 Years**
You are not born with talent; it comes from hard work. Research shows you need to give 10,000 hours of purposeful practice into your profession to become an expert.

72. **Listen & Learn From Others**
A wise piece of advice – "<u>Everyone</u> has something to teach you; if only you would truly listen to them."

73. **Open And Closed Loops**
Un-cram your RAM. A bit like a computer, your brain's Random Access Memory (RAM) quickly fills up. Then, when you have too many "open loops" you cannot think particularly well. This is especially the case at night, when the brain goes through its cleaning, learning and sorting process. So quickly write down the next action step you must take and "close the loop". Then you can move on to the next activity in the daytime, or go back to more restful sleep at night.

74. **Don't try and sleep through the worrying thought**
This problem of "open loops" is especially true when you are stressed and anxious in the middle of the night and are woken worrying about something. Have a small torch, pen and pad of paper by the bed. When you wake worrying, then write the action down and go back to sleep – it will still be there in the morning.

75. **Beware Electronic Irritants**
Never have your mobile phone by your bed as an alarm – you will sleep poorly checking

emails or worrying in case you are called. Try having a curfew hour before sleep when you read a book rather than watch the glare of a screen or TV.

IQ Questions For You

1. How can you make better decisions?

2. How can you stretch yourself and live above the 45 degree line to really learn and grow?

IQ Your Learning & Action

EQ – EMOTIONAL AND SOCIAL INTELLIGENCE

USE YOUR EMOTIONS INTELLIGENTLY. BUILD TRUST AND
RAPPORT SO PEOPLE WILLINGLY WORK FOR YOU.

EQ – Top Tips

Role Archetype: People Motivator

Collaboration
COMMUNICATION
Story-telling
TEAM
CHARACTER
APPRECIATION
VISIBILITY
Discerning
INCLUSIVE
EMPATHY
Accessible
Motivator

76. **Listen Without Needing To Be Right**
Much of the time we are not truly listening
to other people because of our prejudices
and negative judgement. Practise listening to
other people without needing to be right; it
will truly allow you and them to do your finest
thinking.

77. **Invest In Your Emotional Bank Accounts**
It pays to invest relationship energy in your
various stakeholders; don't just transact.
Rather, top up your emotional bank accounts
with each of them by building rapport
and trust. Then when you call on them for
support you have something to draw on.

78. **WIIFM & WAMI**
In a meeting always consider everyone else
present and their perspectives from the point
of view of, "What's In It For Me (WIIFM)?"
and "What's Against My Interests (WAMI)?"

79. **Assumptions**
Ask, "What are we/am I assuming that is
stopping us/me progressing?" Consider the
"un-true limiting assumptions that you are
living as if they are true".

80. **WWW**

Always begin any meeting asking the question, "What is Working Well (WWW) in your work/personal life?" This technique is used in reviews and personal appraisals. You can also end any meeting asking, "What Worked Well in this meeting?"

81. **EBI**

If you're looking to improve situations, where things are not going well, you should ask, "What would make it Even Better If (EBI) we did it?" In that way people are looking for solutions to problems, rather than just complaining about problems.

82. **Be In The Room**

The power of being truly present with someone, by listening to them and being very attentive of what they think, say and do, is significant. So when you are in the room, be IN the room. Don't be on your mobile, or mentally still in the last meeting, or worrying about the next meeting.

83. **Non-Violent Communications (NVC)**

When faced with emotionally charged,

conflict situations, try the NVC approach of
Marshall Rosenberg. Capture the 4 FFCR
steps: Facts, Feelings, Consequences and
my Request.

84. **"Yes And" Rather Than "Yes But"**
If you use a sentence such as, "You've done
a great job, but there were some problems
…" Then do not be surprised if people
forget everything before the BUT and just
remember the criticism that follows it. Is far
more powerful to say "You've done a great
job <u>and</u> what will make it even better would
be if…"

85. **Clear Boundaries & Clear Rules Of Engagement**
The greatest misunderstandings and
problems are caused by a lack of clarity
in meetings and relationships. Be explicit
about your expectations from both sides,
what your boundaries are and your rules of
engagement/ground rules for how your team
will work most effectively together.

86. **Less Is More - Churchill's 1-Page**
Mark Twain apologised, "I am sorry this is a
long letter, if I had spent more time, I would

have written you a short one." Churchill concurred and always insisted on 1-page briefs. Keep your talks to 3 points. Less is more.

87. **Talk More – Email Less**
There is some crucial email etiquette, to save you and others time. Speak to people rather than emailing them. Never blind copy (Bcc) - it "always ends in tears", because you should have been more honest in the first place. People ultimately get to see Bcc email copies that you didn't want them to see.

88. **Appreciation - Catching People Doing Things Right**
Too many leaders are hypercritical: always pointing out what you are doing wrong. Change that by catching people doing things right and say specifically what you appreciate and value about them. Use 3 x Ss - be Specific, Succinct and Sincere.

89. **White Space**
Your job as the leader is to listen at a deep level and understand the white space between the words, the gaps between silos and team members, in order to understand

what's missing and needs to be questioned, or added.

90. **From C2 To "Me Too!"**
Many organisations still prefer a bureaucratic, hierarchical, command and control (C2) structure, with which to run their business. This is an intimidation-based, only good news, fear-of-failure culture. Through coaching, mentoring, empowerment and delegation, inspire your colleagues with powerful stories. Then they will connect with you and your stories, say "me too!" and willingly choose to follow you.

91. **Be A Story Teller**
The power of storytelling is immense. Touch people's emotions, make it personal, share your own story and your vulnerability. Underpin your stories with meaning, values and a clear moral to the story. Powerful Stories = Data + Soul.

92. **Be Empathetic, Whilst Knowing When To Act**
The power of emotional intelligence should never be underestimated; using your empathy to read others is crucial. So too is

Leigh & Jonathan Bowman-Perks MBE

the sense of judgement to know when you have to make tough, unpopular decisions and personally take command, in order to get stalled teams moving forward against tough opposition.

93. **Stimulus & Response**
Between being emotionally triggered (stimulated) by somebody treating you in a specific way and responding to them, you always have choice. Never forget that; you can choose how you manage your reactions. Use your power; don't give it away.

94. **Acceptance To Let Go**
The stoic philosophy has some useful advice. One is that when you have had a bad experience act as if you choose it and then you can live with it. Let go of your irritation and move on in your life.

95. **Commitment: Thumbs Up/ Thumbs Down**
Don't be deceived by the "knowing nod" when you propose a decision. Often such individuals then unravel your decision and disagree with it around the water cooler later on. Instead flush them out to show their

commitment. Get a show of their opinions by actively putting their thumbs in the following positions: up to show support, sideways to show they need more information, or down to show that they are in opposition. You then need to ask those with sideways or down, 'What would it take to make it thumbs up?'

Leigh & Jonathan Bowman-Perks MBE

EQ Questions For You

1. How can you use your emotions more intelligently?

2. Who can you seek out as a peer or direct report and then appreciate qualities about them and their work?

EQ Your Learning & Action

RQ – Resilience

Role Archetype: Resource Mobiliser

RESILIENCE
WILLPOWER
Vulnerable
Successful
Resourceful
Adaptable
Celebration
Perspective

ACTION-ORIENTED

RQ – Top Tips

96. **Mistakes, Learning & Action**
    "Mistakes are inevitable; <u>learning</u> from that experience is <u>optional</u>". Whenever something doesn't work out as you planned, rather than beat yourself up, reflect and ask yourself the question, "What have I learnt and now what can I do differently to be more successful?"

97. **Do Or Do Not – There Is No "Try"**
    "Do or Do Not – there is no Try" - this is the famous response in the film Star Wars from the wise Yoda when Luke Skywalker says he will "give it a try" when doubting his own abilities in the face of huge challenges and adversity.

98. **Face Your Fears - Buffalo Not Cow**
    Fear constricts you both mentally and physically. Laugh at your fear; it has no substance. Apparently when a rainstorm approaches, cows run away from it, being pursued and getting wet and scared for a very long time. Buffaloes, however see the storm coming, turn and face it and charge

at it; quickly running through the rain and beyond into the clear blue sky and sunshine.

99. **I Like Fear – Fear Sets Me Free!**
Consider this 3-step process:
Step 1: Turn and face your own fears - say to yourself, "Bring it on!"
Step 2: say "I like fear"
Step 3: say "Because fear sets me free!"
With such a healthy attitude you realise that your fears and anxieties are just assumptions. They need to be challenged to evaporate and let you get on with doing your real job.

100. **Your Motivation: Towards Or Away From?**
Some people are motivated by fear and getting away from something painful that they don't like. Others are motivated by attraction for an exciting future that they are moving towards. When applying for new jobs, or trying to inspire other people, then be aware that language related to 'towards' is far more energising and attractive to others.

Leigh & Jonathan Bowman-Perks MBE

101. **If We Do Nothing Else We Must...**
It is crucial to decide the purpose of every meeting and that the decision, actions and next steps are agreed at the end. Otherwise, you are wasting your day. To be really focused ask out loud, "If we do nothing else then we must..." Get them to fill in the blank.

102. **Oscillate Between High Performance & Energy Renewal**
Much as you would like to, you cannot be always on and working at top speed and full power. You must find times to replenish and renew your energy sources, both physically and mentally, through giving yourself downtime. This is especially true of having sufficient sleep - ideally 8 hours 36 minutes for the most successful high-performance.

103. **Change Overload & Change Weariness**
Too much continuous change overloads us all, we become weary and very little gets successfully implemented to stand the test of time and be sufficiently sustainable. Take sufficient holidays and completely switch off from work; read, sleep a lot, relax, do

activities and refresh yourself physically and mentally for the challenges when you come back to work.

104. **Positive Attitude To Change**
Winston Churchill had 3 memorable quotes with regards to change:
"When confronted by change, it is better to take it by the hand; if you don't it will take you by the throat!"
"Change is inevitable; resistance is futile".
When criticised for changing his opinion on a very complex situation he replied, "When the situation changes, then I change my opinion. What do you do?"

105. **Speed To Recovery**
As all athletes know, especially business athletes, the fitter you are, then the quicker you recover from intense activity. This is shown most clearly in how quickly you can get your pulse to return to resting heart rate from maximum heart rate.

106. **What Doesn't Kill You, Makes You Stronger**
When you've had a setback, or disappointment, then you need to quickly

bounce back mentally and physically. Ask yourself "What is my learning from this failure, setback, or disappointment?" also ask yourself "What was my part in this failure?" Then take action to redress it.

107. **White-Collar Psychopaths & Sociopaths**
Sadly you will occasionally meet white-collar sociopaths/psychopaths. You need huge resilience in order to not be destroyed by them. First remember you cannot change their toxic behaviour - you will break yourself psychologically trying to do so. They have cold empathy, but no warm empathy and completely lack remorse for their devious ways, lying, distortion and use of other people to achieve their own ends. Keep a record of everything and never expect them to be logical. Do not be a bystander to their toxic and deceitful behaviour and do everything you can to expose them and root them out quickly

108. **Don't Accept Damaging Criticism**
It is crucial to learn from feedback. However, if people try and drag you down with damaging and personally nasty criticism,

remember "feedback" is a gift and if you don't accept it, then it goes back to them; it's THEIR stuff. Sometimes people try and drag you down in order to lift themselves up. Let them keep it and don't own it.

109. **Relax Into Innovation And Success**
Anxious struggling doesn't work. When you are at your most peaceful, calm and relaxed you will find that your best ideas and innovation come to you. You calm your mind, think positively and so generate the vitality hormone DHEA, rather than the stress hormone Cortisol. It is physically and mentally healthier and leads to success.

110. **High Tempo**
The most successful Organisational Leaders have a high tempo-they can maintain momentum, when switching from one direction to a completely new strategic direction. High tempo requires agile, high performing teams to follow such leaders.

111. **Achieve An Early Win**
Nothing breeds more success like success does. We all like to be on a winning team; it's

highly attractive. Set out to achieve small, quick wins to build up confidence and then get bold in your aspirations. Your team will believe they can win again.

112. **Over-Achievers**
If you are an over-achiever, then be prepared to take smaller steps. Then you will build a more resilient, robust and sustainable future. Nature proves that the strongest Hardwood trees put down the deepest roots and grow the most slowly. They can then survive the strongest storms. Trees with shallow roots are blown over and destroyed very quickly. Consequently clarify your MQ, PQ and LQ: be absolutely clear on your values, life meaning and purpose in the legacy you will be leaving.

113. **From Surviving To Thriving**
Step beyond merely surviving and adopt an attitude of thriving in the environment of change, entrepreneurship and tough decision-making.

114. **Rules Of Resilience**
My thanks to my friend Jonathan White an

Ex Royal Marine Officer for The 3 military rules of Resilience:

1. Keep going.
2. Keep calm.
3. Shit happens.

If rule 3 applies refer back to rule 1

Leigh & Jonathan Bowman-Perks MBE

RQ Questions For You

1. How can you show the humility to admit when you need help and don't know the answer?

2. What can you do to recharge and renew more often and not get so depleted that you are overwhelmed by your problems?

RQ Your Learning & Action

WHAT'S YOUR PERSONAL BRAND, REPUTATION AND IMAGE?

BQ - Brand Presence and Impact

BQ

Role Archetype: Brand Promoter

INFLUENCE

Track Record

Brand Alignment

PRESENCE

Visible

Win:Win Oriented

Authentic

NETWORKS

Reputation

Ambassador

Trusted

Politically Savvy

BQ – Top Tips

115. **How Do You Want Others To Feel?**
Always remember –"People will forget what you say, they will forget what you did, but they will never, never forget how you made them <u>feel</u>!" Think ahead to forthcoming meetings and be aware of the impact of your presence and behaviour on how you will make other people feel, especially if you violate their dignity.

116. **Image: 1st Impressions**
A series of experiments by Princeton psychologists Janine Willis and Alexander Todorov reveal that all it takes is 1/10th second to form an impression of a stranger from their face, and that longer exposures don't significantly alter those impressions. So choose carefully the image you wish to portray through what you wear and how you act.

117. **Find Your Voice And Choose Your 3 Key Messages**
Have the courage to find your voice and decide what will be your 3 key messages in

any meeting, or presentation you are giving. Some people take up more time than others and often speak in order to be clear about what they think. Others are reticent to speak and often think long and hard before they decide to speak. Adapt your style.

118. **Power Posing**
Body language affects how others see us, but it may also change how we see ourselves. Social psychologist Amy Cuddy gives a very good TED talk on how "power posing"- standing in a posture of confidence, even when we don't feel confident, can affect testosterone and cortisol levels in the brain, and might even have an impact on our chances for success. Choose your attitude and your body posture.

119. **Body Language**
There is much we can learn about reading body language and being aware of the messages we are unwittingly revealing about ourselves. A Good start point is the book What Every Body is Saying by Ex-FBI agent Joe Navarro. It helps you to better read the "tells", watch for people's baseline

behaviours and then spot anything that is abnormal to indicate whether they're up, down, or potentially lying. A good start point is to study body language.

120. **Authentically You**
People can almost sense someone who is phony and inauthentic; it leads them to be highly suspicious and mistrusting of such people. Oscar Wilde quipped, "be yourself; everyone else is taken!" Further advice on authenticity is, "it is far better to be a 1st-class version of yourself, rather than a 2nd-class version of someone else."

121. **Sponsorship**
Who are your sponsors and ambassadors for your career and your success in your business? Wise and influential sponsors and ambassadors can have a significant influence on your talent development, retention and career opportunities.

122. **Networking**
Be selective in your hyper-busy world and don't just focus on the here and now and what's going on in the next few months.

Think bigger: use networking to learn about future trends, broaden your knowledge, and enrich your experiences. Meet a diverse collection of people. Broaden and share your knowledge and constantly seek out best practice that you can apply to your own role from other sectors and walks of life.

123. **Stakeholder Mapping**
Map out who has power and influence in your organisation and over your career. Then assess your level of visibility and quality of relationship with them. Capture one sheet of how things are now (As Is) and a separate one of the ideal state you would like to move to (To Be) and the actions you need to get there.

124. **How Visible Are You?**
Google your name, see how many entries there are and how many, "hits" are associated with your name and your role. Strengthen your web presence, social media, Twitter, business Facebook account and LinkedIn entries. Be clear on your messages and seek out speaking events and projects where you can contribute your unique

talents.

125. **Begin By Changing Yourself First**
The only person's behaviour you can change is YOUR OWN. Do that first before you give advice, or criticise others. When you change your own behaviour permanently to be a more inspiring leader, then others will change around you for the better too.

126. **Humanity And Humility**
Inspiring leaders always keep their humanity and their humility and are more curious and interesting to others who buy them and all they stand for. This approach is far more successful than people who are self-absorbed, spending time brushing up their ego and overselling themselves by being too absorbed with self-promotion.

127. **Bin PowerPoint!**
Think carefully about your brand, reputation and image when considering presentations and talks. PowerPoint is neither powerful, nor has a point. Don't switch off your audience by thick decks. One page as a handout is best, however if you have to, then keep it to

the smallest number of slides containing the fewest words.

128. **Give Others Credit**
"It is amazing what you can accomplish if you do not care who gets the credit." - President Harry S. Truman.

129. **TNT**
Never underestimate your impact on other people. You are <u>always</u> communicating whether you intend to or not. It is the TNT (Tiny Noticeable Things) that people always remember - about the actions you did, rather than what you said. It's always about the reality they observe, not your aspirational rhetoric. People learn YOU.

130. **Your Boss**
Management tip 101: Don't surprise your boss.
Management Tip 102: Don't surprise your boss's boss.

131. **Vulnerability**
Only the strong, inspiring leaders can be vulnerable. Be prepared to admit your

mistakes and when you don't know, listen and be emotionally open in an appropriate way. It is far more authentic than the leader who bluffs and pretends to know when it's clear they don't.

132. **360 Feedback: What Do People Say About You When You Are Not In The Room?**
One of the greatest barriers to inspiring leadership and success through others is your lack of self-awareness and understanding of your impact on others. Get an independent person to conduct a 360 series of interviews, as well as using a 360-psychometric tool to get feedback on 3 key things: what is working well about you as an inspiring leader; what will make you even better and what people say about you when you're not in the room.

133. **Become Highly influential**
Daniel Priestley advises that if you wish to become a key person of influence there are 5 steps to become highly paid and highly regarded in your industry:

1. Perfect Pitch (succinctly explain who you

are, what you do and where you add value to your clients)

2. Publish (become a published author and consequently an authority on your niche and subject)

3. Profile (through speaking, blogging, videos and becoming known)

4. Products (your intellectual property IP that people value)

5. Partnerships (collaborating with others to your mutual benefit)

BQ Questions For You

1. What did your last 360 feedback tell you? Get an independent person to gather 360 unattributable feedback on you.

2. What is your brand reputation and image?

BQ Your Learning & Action

LEAVE A SUSTAINABLE LEGACY
IN YOUR LIFETIME

LQ

Role Archetype: Universal Steward

Stewardship

LEGACY

VALUE-ADDING
COMMUNITY
Sustainability
Service
Customer
CHARACTER
LONG-TERM

LQ – Top Tips

134. **Added Value?**
Once you have built sufficient trust and respect in your team and firm, then you have earned the right to ask the more courageous questions. One is "where do you add value?' Find out their specific skills and talents that could add real value elsewhere. Ask them where they think they could add true value and move them there. Tapping into your and other people's Passion = Profit.

135. **"Does It Add Value?"**
Use the litmus test of whether an activity adds value to your business and your customers. If it doesn't, don't do it. The Olympic rowers used to ask the question of themselves, "Does it make the boat go faster?" And that was the key test on anything they spent their time on.

136. **Send The Elevator Back Down**
"If you're lucky enough to do well, then it's your responsibility to send the elevator back down" - Kevin Spacey, Actor. When

life has generously rewarded you with good luck and success it's important to use that accumulated financial and experiential wealth to help others too. Positive change in the world doesn't require grand gestures, or extensive planning. Instead, people can promote social benefit in simple, yet effective, ways. Kevin Spacey encouraged others to do just that in the 2000 film "Pay it Forward". Rather than paying people back for their acts of kindness, 'pay it forward' to 2 other people, without expectation of anything in return, other than asking them to repeat the charitable process for 2 others.

137. **Adding To Society Adds To Your Success**
Inspiring leaders add back to society through involvement in charity work and giving of their skills, talent and effort. There is a direct correlation between inspiring leaders and those people who make time to do things which benefit society.

138. **One Degree Of Difference**
Water boils at 100°C. It is extremely hot at 99°C, but it's not producing the steam that we need to turn the turbines. That extra 1°

is what makes such a significant difference. The same is true about you and your performance - that extra 1° makes a huge difference. What will be your extra 1°?

139. **Your Legacy - The Final Countdown**
If you knew you had only 10 minutes to live how would you live now? If you had only 10 hours? If you had only 10 weeks? Or if you had only 10 months? Think about your legacy - you only have this life, so why not live the way you would if you knew you had only a short time left to leave a positive legacy.

140. **Survival, Success, Significance**
It is worth considering whether we are living a life of survival at the base level, a life of success at a higher level, or a life of significance at the pinnacle. Which one are you living?

141. **Memento Mori**
Memento Mori is the Latin phrase for the philosophical reminder about the inevitability of our own death. So we need to reflect on what will be the legacy and what difference

will we make on our short time on this planet.

142. **Would You Choose To Follow Yourself?**
Consider the kind of inspiring leader you are
and spend time to: Prepare and Prevent to
avoid the need for Repair and Repent.

143. **The Mindset You Choose**
William Ward said, "We can throw stones,
complain about them, stumble on them,
climb over them, or build with them." Make
your choice to define the life you lead and
the difference you make.

144. **Be A "Silo Buster"**
When considering your legacy it's important
that you leave your team or organisation
in a better state than you found it. One of
the ways is to develop collaboration and
greater openness with other parts of your
organisation and break down and bust up
silos and small-minded thinking.

145. **Listen Without Needing To Be Right**
A small yet important legacy is the impact
you leave on other people; especially when
you truly listen to them. The problem is

that as humans we often listen from the perspective of needing to be right. The result is we are not truly listening. So practice listening without needing to be right and you will ignite the thinking of the person you are with.

LQ Questions For You

1. What do you want to be your legacy? How would you like people to remember you when you leave your organisation?

2. What would you like people to say about you in your obituary and when they attend your funeral?

3. What charity projects are you currently involved in and how do you give back to society?

LQ Your Learning & Action

RUN PURPOSEFUL, SUCCINCT MEETINGS WITH
CLEAR DECISIONS AND ACTIONS.

About the authors

Leigh and Jonathan Bowman-Perks MBE

Trusted Leadership Advisors, Speakers, Mentor and Coaches for global corporations and their top teams.

Leigh and Jonathan have been described as, "a husband and wife power-couple who share a passion for bringing more inspiring leadership into the world". They are entrepreneurs who founded and run their own inspiring leadership businesses, based on many years' experience. Together they have created The Institute of Inspiring Leadership. They are very proud of their 4 adult children - in the Police, Teaching, Law and Psychology. While Leigh and Jonathan work and live in London and Lincolnshire, they love travelling to help leaders and charity initiatives globally.

Jonathan's vocation has been shaped by his Father's heroic leadership role modelling and his untimely death, as a British Royal Navy fast jet Pilot. His stories and experiences are captured in his book, "Inspiring Leadership; Leadership

Lessons from My Life" (2010)

For her part Leigh published her first book "Inspiring Women Leaders (2014)" which shares her experience and captures a range of stories and wisdom from other inspiring women leaders and the challenges they are facing, have faced and have overcome.

Leigh and Jonathan's life calling is to inspire leaders and teams to:

1. Find and live your "True North" (MQ)
2. Live your life "On Purpose" (PQ)
3. Leave a Legacy (LQ)

They are highly experienced coaches, executive team facilitators, motivational speakers, philanthropists and authors. They focus on current and aspiring CEOs, senior leaders and their teams in all sectors. They partner and collaborate with the best and brightest talent development specialists to support, challenge and inspire leaders around the world.

All profits from their books go to their charity the

Inspiring Leadership Trust helping vulnerable women and children in London, Kenya, Nepal, South Africa and around the world.
Further details are on their websites at:

www.jonathanperks.com
and
www.leighbowmanperks.com

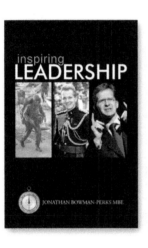

inspiring
LEADERSHIP

JONATHAN BOWMAN-PERKS MBE

INSPIRING
WMEN
LEADERS

LEIGH BOWMAN-PERKS

A HIGHLY PERSONAL INSIGHT INTO THE MINDS OF OVER
100 INSPIRING LEADERS FROM AROUND THE WORLD

Reference books for further reading

50 Years of Research in to EQ. Bar-On, Reuven

Drive: the surprising truth about what motivates us. Pink, Daniel, (2010)

Eat Move Sleep: How Small Choices Lead to Big Changes. Rath, Tom, (2013)

Inferno: the Divine comedy. Kirkpatrick, Robin, & Dante, (2006)

Key Person of Influence: the five-step method to become one of the most highly valued and highly paid people in your industry. Priestley Daniel, (2014)

Man's Search for Meaning: a classic tribute to hope from a survivor of the Holocaust. Frankl, Victor E, (2013)

Nonviolent Communication – A Language of Life. Rosenberg, Marshall, (2015)

Outliers: The Story of Success. Gladwell, Malcolm, (2008)

Quiet: the power of introverts in a world that can't stop talking. Cain, Susan, (2012)

Team of Teams: new rules of engagement for a complex world. McCrystal, Stanley, (2015)

The 7 Habits of Highly Effective People: powerful lessons in personal change. Covey, Stephen R, (2013)

"Penna PLC sponsored Research by Roffey Park in 2003 found that 70% of employees are looking for more 'meaning at work'. Those inspiring leaders who did created 20-30% more discretionary energy."

The Obstacle is the Way: The Ancient Art of Turning Adversity to Advantage. Holiday, Ryan (2015)

The Sign of Enough. Website http://signofenough.com/. Hart, Sara.

The Silo Effect; Why Every Organisation Needs to Disrupt itself in Order to Survive. Tett, Gillian, (2016)

The Speed of Trust: the one thing that changes everything. Covey, Stephen M.R, (2008)

The Tools. Stutz, Phil, (2013)

Time to Think: listening to ignite the human mind. Kline, Nancy, (1999)

What Every BODY is saying; an FBI Agent's Guide to Speed-Reading People. Navarro, Joe, (2008)

Willful Blindness: why we ignore the obvious at our peril. Heffernan, Margaret, (2012)

Some of our clients

Leigh & Jonathan Bowman-Perks MBE

IL-INSPIRING LEADERSHIP

IS YOUR LEADERSHIP STYLE INSPIRING, OR EXPIRING?